AVERY WRIGHT

The Brain in the Machine

Understanding the Inner Workings of Artificial Intelligence

amazon publishing

Contents

Thank You

Dear readers,

I am excited to share my latest book, "The Brain in the Machine: Understanding the Inner Workings of Artificial Intelligence," with you all. It has been a long and rewarding journey to bring this book to life, and I hope it will help you gain a better understanding of the fascinating world of AI.

I want to express my sincere gratitude to everyone who supported me throughout this project. Your encouragement and feedback have been invaluable, and I could not have done it without you.

Thank you for joining me on this journey, and I hope you enjoy the book.

Best regards,

Avery Wright

1

Introduction: Defining AI and Machine Learning

Artificial intelligence (AI) has become a hot topic in recent years as advancements in technology continue to accelerate. AI refers to the ability of machines to perform tasks that typically require human intelligence, such as visual perception, speech recognition, decision-making, and language translation. Machine learning (ML) is a subset of AI that involves the use of algorithms and statistical models to enable machines to learn from data and improve their performance over time.

This book, "The Brain in the Machine: Understanding the Inner Workings of Artificial Intelligence," aims to provide a comprehensive overview of the field of AI and machine learning. The objective of the book is to provide readers with an understanding of the key concepts, techniques, and applications of AI and how it is transforming various industries.

The book is organized into 15 chapters, starting with an introduction that defines AI and machine learning, and provides an overview of the book's objectives. The first chapter also explains key terms and concepts in AI, including neural networks, deep learning, supervised learning, unsupervised learning, and reinforcement learning.

Readers will learn about the history of AI and how it has evolved over time. The book will also explore the various subfields of AI, such as natural language processing, computer vision, robotics, and control systems. Additionally, the book will cover the importance of explainable AI and the ethical concerns and risks associated with AI.

The final chapters of the book will provide readers with an understanding of how to build AI systems, and the tools and frameworks used to train, test, and deploy AI models. The book will also explore the future of AI and the potential impact it could have on society.

Overall, this book is aimed at readers who are interested in gaining a deeper understanding of the inner workings of AI and machine learning. Whether you are a student, researcher, or working professional, this book will provide you with the knowledge and insights needed to stay up-to-date with the latest developments in this exciting and rapidly evolving field.

2

The History of AI

The history of artificial intelligence (AI) dates back to the mid-twentieth century, when researchers first began exploring the possibility of machines that could exhibit human-like intelligence. The concept of AI is rooted in the idea of automating tasks that previously required human cognition, such as logical reasoning, decision-making, and problem-solving.

AI research began in the 1950s with the development of the first electronic computers. In 1956, John McCarthy, Marvin Minsky, Nathaniel Rochester, and Claude Shannon organized a conference at Dartmouth College, which is widely considered the birthplace of AI. At the conference, the researchers proposed that "every aspect of learning or any other feature of intelligence can in principle be so precisely described that a machine can be made to simulate it."

During the 1960s and 1970s, AI research progressed rapidly, with the development of rule-based expert systems, which were used to solve specific problems in fields such as medicine, finance, and engineering. In the 1980s, machine learning algorithms were developed, which enabled machines to learn from data without being explicitly programmed.

The 1990s saw the emergence of neural networks, which are computer systems modeled on the structure and function of the human brain. These systems were used to perform tasks such as speech recognition, natural language processing, and image classification. In the 2000s, deep learning, a subset of machine learning that involves the use of neural networks with multiple layers, revolutionized the field of AI, enabling machines to achieve human-level performance on a range of tasks.

Today, AI is being used in a wide range of applications, from virtual assistants like Siri and Alexa to self-driving cars, facial recognition systems, and medical diagnosis tools. Key milestones in the development of AI include the development of the first chess-playing computer in 1951, the creation of the first chatbot in the 1960s, the first autonomous vehicle in 1984, and the victory of the AI system AlphaGo over a human champion in the game of Go in 2016.

As AI continues to evolve and advance, its potential applications are becoming increasingly diverse and innovative. The history of AI has been a journey of exploration, innovation, and discovery, and it is clear that the field will continue to push the boundaries of what machines can achieve.

3

Neural Networks

Neural networks are a fundamental part of artificial intelligence and are modeled after the structure and function of the human brain. Neural networks are computer systems that are designed to learn and make decisions by processing input data through a series of interconnected nodes, called neurons.

The input data is transformed through the layers of neurons, and the output is a prediction or classification based on the data input. Neural networks are used in a wide range of applications, including image and speech recognition, natural language processing, and autonomous vehicles.

Neural networks are composed of three layers: the input layer, the hidden layer, and the output layer. The input layer receives the data input, which is then processed through the hidden layer, where the computations and transformations occur, before producing the output in the output layer.

Training data is crucial for the success of neural networks. The neural network needs to be trained on a large dataset, to learn patterns, features, and relationships in the data, to be able to generalize the results to new data. During the training phase, the neural network adjusts the weights and biases of each neuron to minimize the error between the predicted output and the actual output.

The activation function is an important aspect of the neural network. The activation function determines the output of each neuron, based on the input it receives. Common activation functions include the sigmoid function, the ReLU function, and the tanh function. Each activation function has its strengths and weaknesses, and choosing the appropriate activation function is an important decision when designing a neural network.

The weights of the neurons are also a crucial component of the neural network. The weights determine the strength of the connection between the neurons in the network, and are used to modify the input signal to produce the desired output. During the training phase, the neural network adjusts the weights to minimize the error and improve the accuracy of the predictions.

4

Deep Learning

Deep learning is a subset of machine learning that involves the use of artificial neural networks with multiple layers to analyze and classify data. Deep learning has revolutionized the field of artificial intelligence, enabling machines to perform complex tasks that were previously thought to be the exclusive domain of humans.

Deep learning is particularly useful for tasks that require large amounts of data and the ability to learn from that data. It can be used to analyze images, speech, text, and other types of data. Deep learning algorithms can automatically learn to recognize patterns in data, enabling machines to make decisions based on that data.

Convolutional Neural Networks (CNNs) are a type of neural network that are particularly well-suited for image analysis. CNNs are designed to detect spatial patterns in images, such as edges and textures, by using a series of filters to scan the image. Each filter produces a feature map that represents the presence of a particular pattern in the image.

Recurrent Neural Networks (RNNs) are a type of neural network that are used for tasks that involve sequences of data, such as speech recognition or natural language processing. RNNs use a feedback loop that allows information to be passed from one step to the next in the sequence, enabling the network to remember information from earlier steps.

Autoencoders are another type of neural network that can be used for tasks such as image and speech recognition. Autoencoders are designed to learn a compressed representation of the input data, which can then be used to reconstruct the original data with a high level of accuracy.

Deep learning has enabled machines to achieve human-level performance on a wide range of tasks, from image classification to speech recognition. The ability of deep learning algorithms to automatically learn and adapt to new data makes it a powerful tool for data analysis and prediction. As we continue to explore the potential of deep learning, we can expect to see new applications and use cases emerge, enabling machines to become even more capable and intelligent.

5

Supervised Learning

Supervised learning is a type of machine learning that involves training an algorithm on a labeled dataset, where each data point is associated with a specific outcome or target variable. The algorithm learns to predict the target variable based on the input features.

In supervised learning, the dataset is divided into a training set and a test set. The training set is used to train the algorithm, and the test set is used to evaluate the performance of the algorithm on new data.

There are two main types of supervised learning problems: classification and regression. Classification is used for predicting a categorical or discrete outcome, while regression is used for predicting a continuous outcome.

Classification problems involve predicting which category a data point belongs to based on its features. Examples of classification problems include email spam detection, image recognition, and fraud detection.

Regression problems involve predicting a continuous value, such as the price of a house or the temperature on a particular day. In regression problems, the algorithm learns to predict a value that is as close as possible to the true value.

Supervised learning algorithms include decision trees, logistic regression, and support vector machines. These algorithms use the input features to make a prediction about the target variable.

The performance of a supervised learning algorithm is measured using evaluation metrics such as accuracy, precision, recall, and F1-score. These metrics measure the performance of the algorithm in terms of its ability to correctly predict the target variable.

6

Unsupervised Learning

Unsupervised learning is a type of machine learning that involves training an algorithm on an unlabeled dataset, where there is no specific target variable. The goal of unsupervised learning is to discover patterns and relationships in the data without any prior knowledge of the outcome.

Unsupervised learning is particularly useful for exploratory data analysis and can be used to identify groups or clusters within the data or detect anomalies that do not fit the expected pattern.

Clustering is a common technique used in unsupervised learning, which involves grouping similar data points together. The objective is to identify clusters of data that share similar features or properties. Clustering algorithms can be used for a wide range of applications, such as customer segmentation, fraud detection, and image segmentation.

Anomaly detection is another technique used in unsupervised learning, which involves identifying data points that do not fit the expected pattern or that are significantly different from the rest of the data. Anomaly detection algorithms can be used for applications such as fraud detection, network intrusion detection, and medical diagnosis.

Common unsupervised learning algorithms include **k-means clustering, hierarchical clustering, and principal component analysis (PCA)**. These algorithms use the features of the data to identify patterns and relationships that are not immediately apparent.

The performance of unsupervised learning algorithms can be difficult to evaluate, as there is no specific target variable to compare the predictions against. However, evaluation metrics such as the silhouette score and the elbow method can be used to evaluate the performance of clustering algorithms.

7

Reinforcement Learning

Reinforcement learning is a type of machine learning that involves training an agent to make decisions based on trial and error. The agent interacts with an environment and learns from the feedback it receives in the form of rewards or punishments. The goal of reinforcement learning is to maximize the cumulative reward over time by making the best decisions based on the feedback it receives.

Reinforcement learning is particularly useful for tasks that involve decision-making in complex, dynamic environments, such as robotics, game playing, and autonomous vehicles.

The agent learns through a process of trial and error, where it takes an action in the environment and receives feedback in the form of a reward or punishment. The agent then adjusts its behavior to maximize the reward it receives in the future.

The reinforcement learning process involves three main components: the agent, the environment, and the reward signal. The agent is the decision maker that interacts with the environment, which is the world in which the agent operates. The reward signal is the feedback the agent receives for its actions in the environment, which may be positive or negative.

The agent learns through a process of exploration and exploitation. In the exploration phase, the agent tries out different actions to learn more about the environment and the rewards associated with different actions. In the exploitation phase, the agent uses the knowledge it has gained to make the best decisions based on the rewards it expects to receive.

Common reinforcement learning algorithms include **Q-learning, policy gradients, and actor–critic methods**. These algorithms use a combination of exploration and exploitation to learn the optimal policy for the agent to follow.

The performance of reinforcement learning algorithms is evaluated based on their ability to maximize the cumulative reward over time. This is often measured using a metric called the return, which is the total reward earned over a given time horizon.

8

Natural Language Processing

Natural Language Processing (NLP) is a field of artificial intelligence that focuses on the interaction between computers and human language. NLP is used to analyze, understand, and generate human language, and has a wide range of applications, including chatbots, speech recognition, machine translation, and sentiment analysis.

NLP is used to analyze and understand the structure and meaning of language, and to transform unstructured data into structured data that can be used by machines. NLP can be used to extract meaning from text, identify patterns and relationships, and even generate new text.

Sentiment analysis is a common application of NLP that involves analyzing text to determine the sentiment or emotion expressed in the text. Sentiment analysis is used for a wide range of applications, including social media monitoring, market research, and customer service.

Machine translation is another common application of NLP, which involves translating text from one language to another. Machine translation is used for applications such as website localization, international communication, and language learning.

Question answering is a type of NLP that involves answering questions posed in natural language. Question answering is used for applications such as customer service, search engines, and virtual assistants.

NLP techniques include tasks such as text classification, entity recognition, and part-of-speech tagging. These tasks are used to analyze the structure and meaning of language, and to extract information from unstructured data.

Common NLP tools and frameworks include NLTK, spaCy, and TensorFlow. These tools provide a range of functions and features that can be used for a wide range of NLP tasks.

The performance of NLP algorithms is evaluated based on their ability to accurately analyze and understand human language. Evaluation metrics include precision, recall, and F1-score, which measure the performance of the algorithm in terms of its ability to correctly classify and extract information from text.

9

Computer Vision

Computer vision is a field of artificial intelligence that focuses on enabling machines to interpret and analyze visual data. Computer vision is used for applications such as image and video processing, autonomous vehicles, and robotics.

Computer vision is used to analyze and understand the content of images and videos, and to identify objects, people, and other features of the visual world.

Object detection is a common application of computer vision that involves identifying and locating objects within an image or video. Object detection is used for applications such as surveillance, autonomous vehicles, and robotics.

Image segmentation is another application of computer vision that involves dividing an image into multiple segments, each of which represents a different object or region of the image. Image segmentation is used for applications such as medical imaging, satellite imagery analysis, and autonomous vehicles.

Facial recognition is a type of computer vision that involves identifying and verifying the identity of a person based on their facial features. Facial recognition is used for applications such as security and surveillance, authentication, and access control.

Computer vision techniques include tasks such as feature detection, feature extraction, and image classification. These tasks are used to analyze and understand the content of images and videos.

Common computer vision tools and frameworks include **OpenCV, TensorFlow, and PyTorch**. These tools provide a range of functions and features that can be used for a wide range of computer vision tasks.

The performance of computer vision algorithms is evaluated based on their ability to accurately identify and analyze visual data. Evaluation metrics include accuracy, precision, and recall, which measure the performance of the algorithm in terms of its ability to correctly classify and analyze images and videos.

10

Robotics and Control

Artificial intelligence is a key component of modern robotics and control systems, enabling machines to make decisions, learn from their environment, and interact with the world in a more intelligent and responsive manner. Robotics and control systems are used for a wide range of applications, from manufacturing and logistics to healthcare and entertainment.

AI is used in robotics and control systems to enable machines to perform tasks that are difficult or impossible for humans to do, such as lifting heavy objects, navigating complex environments, and performing precise movements with extreme accuracy.

Motion planning and control is a key technique used in robotics and control systems, which involves planning and controlling the motion of the robot in response to its environment. Motion planning and control are used for tasks such as grasping, manipulation, and navigation, and are essential for enabling robots to interact with the world in a safe and efficient manner.

Decision-making algorithms are another key technique used in robotics and control systems, which involve making decisions based on data and feedback from the environment. Decision-making algorithms are used for tasks such as path planning, object recognition, and obstacle avoidance, and are essential for enabling robots to make intelligent decisions in complex and dynamic environments.

Common robotics and control systems tools and frameworks include **ROS (Robot Operating System), Gazebo, and V-REP**. These tools provide a range of functions and features that can be used for a wide range of robotics and control tasks.

The performance of robotics and control systems is evaluated based on their ability to accurately and efficiently perform tasks, such as grasping, manipulation, and navigation. Evaluation metrics include accuracy, efficiency, and safety, which measure the performance of the system in terms of its ability to successfully perform the task at hand.

11

Explainable AI

Explainable AI (XAI) is a field of artificial intelligence that focuses on making the decisions and actions of machine learning algorithms more transparent and understandable to human users. The goal of XAI is to enable humans to understand how and why machine learning algorithms are making certain decisions, and to provide insights into their inner workings.

The importance of XAI lies in its ability to enable human users to trust and validate the output of machine learning algorithms, and to identify and correct errors or biases in the decision-making process.

Key techniques used in XAI include **feature visualization, model interpretation, and counterfactual analysis**. Feature visualization involves visualizing the features or inputs that are most important to the algorithm, and can help to identify and understand the patterns and relationships in the data that the algorithm is using to make decisions.

Model interpretation involves analyzing the structure and parameters of the model to understand how it is making decisions. Model interpretation techniques can help to identify and explain the decision-making process, and can provide insights into how the model can be improved or optimized.

Counterfactual analysis involves analyzing the impact of changing the input or features of the data on the output of the algorithm. Counterfactual analysis can help to identify how and why certain decisions are being made, and can provide insights into how the algorithm can be improved or optimized.

Common XAI tools and frameworks include **SHAP (Shapley Additive Explanations), LIME (Local Interpretable Model-Agnostic Explanations), and Anchor.** These tools provide a range of functions and features that can be used to explain and interpret the output of machine learning algorithms.

The performance of XAI algorithms is evaluated based on their ability to accurately and transparently explain the output of machine learning algorithms. Evaluation metrics include accuracy, transparency, and interpretability, which measure the performance of the algorithm in terms of its ability to provide meaningful and understandable explanations of the output.

12

Ethics and Bias in AI

As artificial intelligence and machine learning continue to advance, it is important to consider the ethical implications of these technologies. AI has the potential to transform many aspects of our lives, but it also poses significant ethical challenges and risks.

Some of the ethical concerns surrounding AI and machine learning include issues such as **privacy, security, and accountability**. There is a risk that these technologies could be misused or abused, and there is a need to ensure that they are used in a responsible and ethical manner.

One of the most significant risks of AI and machine learning is the potential for bias and discrimination. AI systems can inadvertently perpetuate or amplify existing biases and discrimination in society, based on the data used to train them. This can have significant impacts on individuals and groups who are already marginalized or disadvantaged.

For example, facial recognition algorithms have been shown to have higher error rates for people with darker skin tones, and language translation algorithms have been shown to perpetuate gender stereotypes. These biases can have significant real-world consequences, such as false accusations and wrongful arrests, and can reinforce existing prejudices and discrimination.

To address these ethical concerns, it is important to ensure that AI and machine learning systems are designed and deployed in a responsible and ethical manner. This can involve using diverse and representative data sets, evaluating and mitigating bias and discrimination, and ensuring transparency and accountability in the decision-making process.

Common techniques for addressing bias and discrimination in AI systems include **data cleaning and preprocessing, algorithmic fairness and transparency, and diverse and representative training data.** These techniques can help to ensure that AI systems are fair, transparent, and accountable.

The performance of AI systems is evaluated based on their ability to make unbiased and ethical decisions, while minimizing the risk of discrimination and harm. Evaluation metrics include fairness, accuracy, and accountability, which measure the performance of the system in terms of its ability to make fair and responsible decisions.

13

Building AI Systems

Building artificial intelligence systems requires a wide range of tools and frameworks, including programming languages, libraries, and software platforms. These tools and frameworks are used to design, train, test, and deploy machine learning models for a wide range of applications.

One of the most popular programming languages for building AI systems is Python, which has a wide range of libraries and frameworks for machine learning and data science, such as **TensorFlow, PyTorch, and Scikit-learn**. These libraries provide a range of functions and features for tasks such as data preprocessing, model selection, and evaluation.

Other commonly used tools and frameworks for building AI systems include data storage and management systems, such as Apache Hadoop and Apache Spark, which are used for processing and analyzing large datasets. Cloud computing platforms, such as Amazon Web Services and Microsoft Azure, provide tools for building, training, and deploying machine learning models at scale.

To build an AI system, it is necessary to have a clear understanding of the problem domain and the data that will be used to train the model. This involves identifying the features or inputs that are most relevant to the task, and preparing the data to ensure that it is clean, consistent, and representative of the problem domain.

Once the data has been prepared, the next step is to select and train a machine learning model. This involves selecting an appropriate algorithm and architecture for the task, and training the model on the data using techniques such as supervised, unsupervised, or reinforcement learning.

Once the model has been trained, it is important to evaluate its performance using appropriate metrics such as accuracy, precision, and recall. This can involve testing the model on a separate validation dataset, and comparing its performance to other models or benchmarks.

Finally, the model can be deployed in a production environment, where it can be used to make predictions or decisions in real-time. This involves integrating the model into a larger software system or application, and ensuring that it is reliable, scalable, and maintainable.

14

Future of AI

Artificial intelligence is a rapidly evolving field, with new advances and innovations emerging on a regular basis. The potential applications and impact of AI in the future are vast, and have the potential to transform many aspects of our lives.

One area where AI is likely to have a significant impact is healthcare. AI can be used for tasks such as medical diagnosis, drug discovery, and personalized medicine, and has the potential to improve the accuracy and efficiency of healthcare systems.

Another area where AI is likely to have a significant impact is transportation. AI can be used for tasks such as traffic management, route planning, and autonomous vehicles, and has the potential to improve the safety and efficiency of transportation systems.

AI is also likely to have a significant impact on the workplace, with the potential to automate many tasks and increase productivity. This could lead to significant changes in the workforce, with a shift towards jobs that require creativity, problem-solving, and interpersonal skills.

Current research and trends in AI development include areas such as reinforcement learning, generative models, and natural language processing. Reinforcement learning involves enabling agents to learn through trial and error, and has the potential to enable machines to learn and adapt in real-time.

Generative models involve creating new data based on existing data, and have the potential to be used for tasks such as image and video generation, and natural language processing. Natural language processing involves enabling machines to understand and generate human language, and has the potential to transform communication and information processing.

As AI continues to evolve and advance, it is important to consider the ethical implications and risks associated with these technologies. It is important to ensure that AI is developed and deployed in a responsible and ethical manner, with a focus on transparency, accountability, and the protection of individual rights and freedoms.

15

Conclusion: The Impact of AI

Artificial intelligence has the potential to transform many aspects of our lives, from healthcare and transportation to the workplace and beyond. The impact of AI on society is significant, with the potential for both positive and negative outcomes.

On the positive side, AI can be used to improve efficiency, productivity, and safety in many areas of life. It can enable faster and more accurate decision-making, and can help us to solve complex problems that would otherwise be difficult or impossible to solve.

On the negative side, AI can also perpetuate and amplify existing biases and discrimination, and there is a risk that these technologies could be misused or abused. There is also a risk that AI could displace jobs and exacerbate economic inequality.

It is important to recognize that the impact of AI is not predetermined, and that it will depend on how these technologies are developed and deployed. It is important to prioritize responsible

AI development and ethical use of AI technologies, with a focus on transparency, accountability, and the protection of individual rights and freedoms.

This includes ensuring that AI systems are developed and trained using diverse and representative data, and that they are evaluated and optimized for fairness and accuracy. It also involves ensuring that AI systems are transparent and accountable in their decision-making processes, and that they are designed to protect individual privacy and security.

As individuals, organizations, and societies, we have a responsibility to ensure that AI is developed and used in a responsible and ethical manner, with a focus on the well-being of individuals and society as a whole. This requires a commitment to ongoing education, research, and collaboration, and a willingness to adapt and evolve as new challenges and opportunities emerge.

16

Glossary

Artificial intelligence (AI) - The simulation of human intelligence in machines that are programmed to think and learn like humans.

Artificial general intelligence (AGI) - A hypothetical form of AI that would be capable of performing any intellectual task that a human can.

Artificial neural network - A type of machine learning algorithm that is inspired by the structure and function of the human brain.

Backpropagation - A method for training artificial neural networks that involves adjusting the weights of the network based on the error between the predicted and actual outputs.

Computer vision - A field of AI that focuses on enabling machines to understand and interpret visual information.

Convolutional neural network - A type of neural network that is designed for processing and analyzing images.

Deep learning - A type of machine learning that involves training neural networks with many layers, allowing them to learn increasingly complex features and representations.

Explainable AI - A field of AI that focuses on making the decisions and actions of machine learning algorithms more transparent and understandable to human users.

Hyperparameter - A parameter in a machine learning model that is set before training begins and controls the behavior of the model during training.

Machine learning - The use of algorithms and statistical models to enable machines to improve their performance on a task over time.

Natural language processing (NLP) - A field of AI that focuses on enabling machines to understand and generate human language.

Recurrent neural network - A type of neural network that is designed for processing and analyzing sequences of data, such as time series or natural language.

Reinforcement learning - A type of machine learning where an agent learns through trial and error, receiving rewards or punishments for its actions.

Supervised learning - A type of machine learning where the algorithm is trained on labeled data, with the goal of predicting the labels of new, unseen data.

Transfer learning - A technique in machine learning where a pre-trained model is used as a starting point for a new, related task, allowing for faster and more efficient training.

Unsupervised learning - A type of machine learning where the algorithm is trained on unlabeled data, with the goal of identifying patterns and relationships in the data.

17

Additional Resources

The following are some additional resources for those interested in learning more about artificial intelligence:

The AI Index: an annual report on the state of artificial intelligence, produced by the Stanford Institute for Human-Centered AI.

The AI Ethics Lab: a nonprofit organization focused on promoting responsible and ethical AI development and deployment.

The Responsible AI Institute: an organization focused on promoting responsible and ethical AI development and deployment.

The Future of Life Institute: a nonprofit organization focused on ensuring that AI is developed and used in a responsible and beneficial manner.

The Association for Computing Machinery: a professional organization for computer scientists and other computing professionals, with a focus on AI and related areas.

18

References

[1] Goodfellow, Ian, Yoshua Bengio, and Aaron Courville. Deep Learning. MIT Press, 2016.

[2] Russell, Stuart J., and Peter Norvig. Artificial Intelligence: A Modern Approach. Pearson Education, 2010.

[3] Chollet, François. Deep Learning with Python. Manning Publications, 2017.

[4] Murphy, Kevin P. Machine Learning: A Probabilistic Perspective. MIT Press, 2012.

[5] Domingos, Pedro. The Master Algorithm: How the Quest for the Ultimate Learning Machine Will Remake Our World. Basic Books, 2015.

About the Author

Avery Wright is an enigmatic figure who is an author in the fields of AI, Technology, and the Arts. A combat veteran of the US Army, Avery has almost two decades of experience in the IT industry, which has given them a unique perspective on the intersection of technology and society.

As an author, Avery has published a range of books on topics such as the future of AI, the role of drones in modern warfare, and the medicinal properties of mushrooms. Their writing often explores the cutting-edge of technology and how it is changing the world around us. Avery's work is notable for its depth and insight, as well as its ability to make complex topics accessible to a broad audience.

Away from the world of writing, Avery is a private individual who values their privacy. Despite this, they remain a voice in the tech industry and beyond. Whether sharing their thoughts on the latest developments in AI or commenting on the state of the world, Avery's perspective is always worth listening to.

You can connect with me on:

🌐 https://sirexodia.wixsite.com/avery-wright

🐦 https://twitter.com/AveryWrightAI

f https://www.facebook.com/profile.php?id=100089987171726

🖉 https://www.amazon.com/author/averywrightai

Subscribe to my newsletter:

✉ https://sirexodia.wixsite.com/avery-wright

Also by Avery Wright

Also by Avery Wright
  "Mastering Midjourney AI: The Beginner's Handbook"
  "Chat GPT: A Digital Journey Begins"
  "AI and the Art of Binary"
  "Mycological Marvels: Exploring the Art of AI-Created Mushrooms"
  "AI in Healthcare: How Artificial Intelligence is Transforming Medicine"
  "Transformative Art:: A Journey with Artificial Intelligence"
  "From Predator to Phantom: A Glimpse At Drones"
  "AI and the Future of Humanity"
  "The Tao of Inner Peace"
  "Taoism Unleashed: Advanced Concepts for Deepening Your Practice"
  "The Knife's Edge:: A View on the Ultra Rich and their Motivations"
  "Defending the Skies: The Rise of Unidentified Aerial Phenomena and the Battle for Airspace Dominance"
  "Mastering the Board: The Power of Pawns in Chess"
  "The Brain in the Machine: Understanding the Inner Workings of Artificial Intelligence"
  "Healing with Fungi: The Science of Medicinal Mushrooms"
  "Chat GPT: ChatGPT Explores the World: Conversations Across Cultures"
  "Chat GPT: Unleashing ChatGPT's Power: Navigating the Digital Realm"

Avery Wright's work spans a range of topics, from the cutting-edge of AI and technology to the ancient practice of Taoism and the art of chess. Their books are notable for their depth, insight, and ability to make complex topics accessible to a broad audience. With almost two decades of experience in the IT field and a background as a combat veteran, Avery brings a unique perspective to their writing that is both informative and thought-provoking. Whether you are interested in exploring the frontiers of technology or deepening your understanding of the human experience, Avery's books are a must-read.

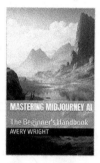

Mastering Midjourney AI - The Beginner's Handbook
Mastering Midjourney AI: The Beginner's Handbook is a comprehensive guide for beginners looking to learn about the Midjourney AI platform and how to use it for image generation. The book covers a range of topics, including understanding Midjourney AI's parameters and settings, using URLs for image inspiration, adjusting image quality, and more.
https://www.amazon.com/dp/B0BV8PGDXT

Transformative Art - A Journey with Artificial Intelligence

Transformative Art: A Journey with AI is a visually stunning and thought-provoking book that explores the intersection of artificial intelligence and the world of art. The book features breathtaking images of futuristic cities, technology, vehicles, robots, flying ships, conceptual art, abstract art, and unique pieces, all within the context of transformative art. Each chapter begins with a powerful quote that sets the tone for a deep dive into the themes of perception, change, reflection, risk-taking, emotional connection, the journey within, and the universal language of art. The book is written by Avery Wright, a talented author with a passion for exploring the ways in which technology is changing our lives and our world. This book is a must-read for anyone interested in the intersection of art, technology, and the human experience. https://www.amazon.com/dp/B0BTWNYLJD

AI and the Art of Binary

"Binary and AI: The Art of Computer Science" delves into the world of binary and its applications in artificial intelligence. The book starts with an explanation of binary and its relationship with computer science, followed by an in-depth exploration of the different applications of binary in AI, including machine learning, natural language processing, computer vision, and robotics. The book also covers the coding aspect of binary for AI and provides the reader with best practices and tools used for coding.

https://www.amazon.com/dp/B0BV5RK9ZG

AI in Healthcare: How Artificial Intelligence is Transforming Medicine

Discover the groundbreaking impact of AI in healthcare. From personalized medicine to revolutionizing the healthcare workforce, AI is changing the game. Get a deeper understanding of its current and future applications and the ethical, legal, and social implications in "AI in Healthcare: How Artificial Intelligence is Transforming Medicine." Get your copy now on Amazon!
https://www.amazon.com/dp/B0BTBZDVBY

www.ingramcontent.com/pod-product-compliance
Lightning Source LLC
LaVergne TN
LVHW051751050326
832903LV00029B/2852